Metallica
TheClubDayz

Metallica
TheClubDayz
Live, raw and without a photo pit!

by **BILL HALE**

Additional text by **BOB NALBANDIAN**

ECW Press

Dedicated to Cliff Burton
(Miss ya, Buddy)

Cheers to Lars, James, Ron, Kirk, Jason
and Dave for always letting me do my thing!
To all the fans, new and old, of Metallica . . .
To this lifestyle we call rock and roll . . .
To my old friends: John (St. Red) Strednansky,
Ron Quintana, Scott Earl and Bob Nalbandian . . .
Thanks for keeping this music alive!
To my "Sunday Ohana," for always being there . . .
Thanks to my Mom and Pops . . . Love ya!
Big Hugs and Kisses to Reecie, Ayslee,
Jamin and Tari Mahaloz for the support!

Copyright © William Hale, 2009

Published by ECW Press, 2120 Queen Street East, Suite 200,
Toronto, Ontario, Canada M4E 1E2 / 416.694.3348 / info@ecwpress.com

All rights reserved. No part of this publication may be reproduced, stored
in a retrieval system, or transmitted in any form by any process — electronic,
mechanical, photocopying, recording, or otherwise — without the prior
written permission of the copyright owners and ECW Press.

LIBRARY AND ARCHIVES CANADA CATALOGUING IN PUBLICATION

Hale, Bill
Metallica: the club dayz 1982-1984 / Bill Hale.

ISBN-13 978-1-55022-876-2
ISBN-10 1-55022-876-5

1. Metallica (Musical group)—Pictorial works. I. Title. II. Title: Club dayz.

ML421.M587H16 2009   782.421660922   C2008-907555-2

Editor: Jennifer Hale
Cover design: David Gee
Interior layout and design: Tania Craan
Printing: Transcontinental

PRINTED AND BOUND IN CANADA

ECW PRESS
ecwpress.com

It was in Oakland,
at a Judas Priest concert,
when my life changed...

Oakland, California, 1981. . . . A Judas Priest concert changed my life. Not in the way others may say they felt the first time they saw a particular heavy metal band live. In fact, Judas Priest had little to do with it. But my life did change. A few days after the concert I was at home when my phone rang. Some kid with an accent was on the other end asking me where in the world I found that cool satin Iron Maiden jacket he saw me wearing at that gig. He claimed to be a huge fan of not only Iron Maiden and Judas Priest, but all English heavy metal, especially the New Wave of British Heavy Metal. Who was this guy?

I myself had long discovered the famed NWOBHM by then. My record collection was quickly filling up with up 'n' coming artists like Tygers of Pan Tang, Angel Witch, Fist, A II Z, Girlschool, Motörhead and of course, Diamond Head. So we hit it off right away. The voice on the other end of that phone call belonged to a young metal fan named Lars Ulrich.

Our discussions quickly became more frequent and regular. Lars started to call me weekly from his job at a Los Angeles gas station. I still grin when I remember Lars telling me about the new Sledgehammer single in between his screams at a customer to "Use pump #7 and not 8!" We also began to exchange tapes, records and 45s of lesser-known British and European bands. Great stuff. One night he played me Accept's "Fast as a Shark" over the phone, the first time I ever heard that classic song! Looking back, even today I am still grateful to Lars for introducing me to so many cool bands out of Europe. I have been known to be a slut for Euro-metal ever since!

Eventually, anyone who loved metal as much as Lars Ulrich would want to start their own band. Lars was excited when the time came, but what would this new band be called? The metal community now knows that he "stole" the name from the San Francisco fanzine published by Ron Quintana. Quintana was going to call his new magazine "Metallica." Lars, quick on the trigger, talked Ron into naming it "Metal Mania" — reserving the name Metallica for his plans for world domination.

In the early days of Metallica, the band, I was often a welcome visitor to rehearsals via phone connection. Listening over an open phone line from 300 miles away, I was one of the first to hear the beginnings of such masterpieces as "Hit the Lights," "Whiplash" and "Seek and Destroy." Even during these early days, James, Lars and then-members Dave Mustaine and Ron McGovney were amazing songwriters and musicians. I couldn't wait to see them live.

Their first concert in San Francisco finally took place in 1982. I talked them into stopping by my home in Monterey to meet me so we could drive up together. Lars rode in the back of my white Mercury Capri and we blasted loud music all the way

to the Stone in downtown SF. Stories describing this first gig are abundant and documented — it was truly a historical event!

The next key event in the early life of Metallica happened as they prepared additional shows in the Bay Area. Lars called me and started to rave about this incredible bass player he watched perform the night before in Hollywood. I was already aware that the band was thinking about replacing Ron and once Lars saw Cliff Burton, he was hooked! I had met Cliff several months prior at the San Francisco Waldorf when he performed with his band Trauma at "Metal Mondays" and we became friends. I gave Lars Cliff's number but he was too hesitant to call himself. So he asked me to arrange a meeting with Cliff in San Francisco and I obliged. The rest, once again, is history . . .

The two years that followed saw Metallica get all the breaks they truly deserved.

What started with their appearance on the legendary *Metal Massacre* compilation was soon followed by the trip and ensuing New York recording session and *Megaforce* contract, the historic *Kill 'Em All* album debut, a sold-out national tour with Raven and other famed bands, and finally their breakthrough deal with Elektra Records. Through all of this, the guys were starving and survived through Lars selling his precious 45s and other NWOBHM records to yours truly. More importantly, they successfully managed to replace guitarist Dave Mustaine with Kirk Hammett and expand their fan base across the planet with non-stop touring, blinding shows and eager press coverage wherever they went. Metallica's loyal fans never stopped being important to this band.

But once the Elektra deal was sealed, the loyal fans who supported the band since the beginning knew that Metallica was soon to become the biggest hard rock band in the world. Now, almost 30 years later, it still is. Up the irons, Lars! It's a long way from those gas station days to the mansions above San Francisco Bay.

Keep Listening and Keep Living the Metal Spirit,
John Strednansky
Editor and Chief of *Metal Rendezvous Int*.
Heavy Rock–Metal Magazine

Metallica, March 1983
Stone Shows: A Total Recall

The March 1983 Metallica concerts at the Stone in San Francisco were the culmination of six months of violent pummeling of Northern California Metalheads in an attack that has no equal in history. It all began rather innocently, with a Metal Blade Records *Metal Massacre* invasion, featuring some of L.A.'s promising up-and-coming metal bands, at the Stone on September 18, 1982. When Cirith Ungol dropped out as the opening act for typical southland hard rock band Bitch, Metal Blade main man Brian Slagel invited Metallica to play in Ungol's place. They opened and blew the headliners away. The ferocious pounding the SF audience got that night and the surprisingly warm reception they gave Metallica would soon change both the band and area metal fans forever.

Concerts on October 18 and November 29 at the Old Waldorf continued the onslaught. Metallica's fourth show in the City was the "Metal Mania Massacre Benefit Party" at the world famous Mabuhay Gardens on November 30. It became Metallica bassist Ron McGovney's last gig. He later drove the band home to L.A. one last tormented time. James Hetfield, Lars Ulrich and Dave Mustaine had convinced Cliff Burton to join their unholy trio. He would quit his band Trauma, but in return they would have to give up Hollywood. They wasted absolutely no time and soon headed north to the Bay Area.

From December '82 through February '83 James and Lars were moving into Exodus manager Mark Whittaker's small house on Carlson Boulevard in El Cerrito. The pad soon became infamous as the "MetalliMansion," with Dave being forced to live in the back of Mark's granny's house! On December 28, Cliff arrived to jam for the very first time with the boys in the small, barely soundproofed "MetalliGarage" off in the corner of Mark's property. The guys would later say that first jam was pure magic. The new Metallica would reconvene over the next three months to practice both music and con-suming mass quantities of booze. They would also often check out local metal shows.

The next Metal Mania Benefit at the Mabuhay took place February 20, just two weeks prior to the heavily advertised Stone shows in March. Every pole and bulletin board in the Bay Area had at least three black and yellow Metallica/Lääz Rockit/Exodus posters plastered to it and everyone and their brother were passing them out at shows. At the benefit, half the Mab was covered in yellow and black! Exodus was support-ing Anvil Chorus that night and during their encore James, Dave and Lars jumped onstage during guitarist Kirk Hammett's solo and proceeded to thrash and headbang like maniacs begging for whiplash before being herded off by the "Slay Team" security gang. It was Metallica's first time on stage with Kirk Hammett.

Metallica had been together barely a year yet had four very

popular demos floating around. There were the Ron McGovney Garage (Daze?) demos cheaply recorded with several cover songs, the four-song monster misnamed *Power Metal* and the definitive seven-song masterpiece *No Life 'til Leather*. The fourth demo, *Metal Up Your Ass*, was recorded on a boom box at November's Old Waldorf show and sounded like shit, but was so blazingly raw and over-the-top everyone had to have it!

During this time I was the deejay for KUSF's "Rampage Radio" and I was playing the official demos plus various 'Talica bootlegs weekly, if not hourly, from 2 a.m. until 8 a.m. on the Saturday night shift. Often on those early Sunday mornings James, Lars or Dave would drop in (usually with a plentiful amount of vodka!) and yell about their upcoming concerts. They would hype up their gigs, play their favorite metal songs and slag off certain bands for being "poseurs," especially the irrepressible (and usually drunk) Dave. They swore so fucking much I even got suspended for a time by KUSF due to complaints! But they were always entertaining and never too out of control.

Lars liked to deejay and explore the station's extensive library while Dave and James loved talking to the callers and asking them questions as well as being questioned themselves. Cliff was still the "new guy" at that time, living farther south in Castro Valley and not coordinating his partying with his new bandmates.

By March, most local hardcore metalheads had bought or traded Metallica tapes and knew the nine originals by heart (as well as the cover tunes) and were more than ready to sing along come the return of the new and improved Metallica.

On Saturday March 5, 1983, Broadway Avenue in San Francisco was buzzing in yellow and black. Denim, leather, buttons, patches and pegged jeans were everywhere. The Stone was swarmed with headbangers who'd bought their priceless $5 tickets in hopes of deadly disembowelment (with extreme prejudice) by the nuclear bands that night. First onstage were the deadly quintet Exodus, which featured rabid guitarists Kirk Hammett and Gary Holt, the Bay Area's pre-eminent drummer Tom Hunting, and one of the funniest front men in the world, Paul Baloff. They were always trying to be the fastest, tightest, noisiest and nastiest band in town. They often were, but now these southern upstarts Metallica had moved into their neighborhood, borrowed their manager and challenged Exodus as the Bay's heaviest band. That was not acceptable to Paul and the gang as they tore through classic rippers like "Piranha," "Die by the Sword" (which Kirk later remolded into "Creeping Death"), and the amazing "Impaler." Technically, Kirk and Gary played more challenging riffs and harmonies than Dave and James, while Baloff was just this amazing front-guy — a hairy cannonball of a screamer often inciting crowds with cries of "Kill All Poseurs!" In concert Exodus was a stunning napalm attack of sight and sound.

Next up was the Bay Area's most popular metal group, Lääz Rockit. They were a whirlwind of promotion and gigging with a Judas Priest–meets–Iron Maiden vibe. Hard and heavy and more polished than their noisy bill-mates, Lääz were tight in their heavy leather outfits. They were leaders of the East Bay scene, but would soon be dethroned by thrashier groups like the ones they shared the stage with this night. The writing was on the wall.

As an overabundance of fog engulfed the stage, Metallica proceeded to start their show with a bombast of feedback and double-bass drumming that launched into "Hit the Lights." Thrash-as-fast-as-the-speed-of-light was the theme as Dave, James, Lars and now Cliff were in their purest form. The manic foursome played as fast as inhumanly possible while James yelped "HE-YIT DA LIE-EYE-YITSSS!" in the highest register he had ever hit (or would ever hit, for that matter!). The crowd went insane. The music scene of the Bay Area (and the world, for that matter) would never be the same.

As the thundering tune crashed to a halt, James exclaimed to the crowd, "How you doing? We're ready to Fucking KILL!"

before launching into Dave Mustaine's "The Mechanix." The cataclysmic ditty pounded along for the last time as "The Mechanix" (as a few months later James would morph it into "The Four Horsemen") as the crowd slowly and inexorably began to focus their attention to the left of the stage.

Right there stood the thing that could not be . . . head-banging, thrashing, violently assaulting his bass and making otherworldly sounds come out of it that had never been heard by human ears. Not at a metal show; not at any concert! There he was making these insane runs and fills while wailing and wracking his Rickenbacker ever so rudely. I'd seen Cliff Burton at an occasional practice and I'd seen him in his previous band Trauma, but Trauma never unleashed him like this. Cliff was awesome, a genius madman and a show unto himself.

"The next one is dedicated to the new rager Cliff Burton. It's called 'Phantom Lord,'" exclaimed James before bolting into the song. After that monster came Mustaine's "Jump in the Fire" (James would shortly change its lyrics too) as Lars pounded out a crushing beat, practically kicking in his newly purchased double-bass kit. The little guy pulverized his kit recklessly as the rest of the group furiously thrashed alongside as the audience's heads and fists were flying along to the beat of the "FIIIE-YAAAAHH!!"

"This song is about living hard . . . 'Motorbreath'!" James exclaimed. It sounded like the four madmen had launched a nuclear missile! The audience was spazzing out in all directions, but mostly gasping for air as they tried to catch their breath throughout the assault. Luckily, Dave broke a chord in all the commotion, saying "Why am I the only one who fucks up?" Alas, we all caught a break . . . and our breath.

"'No Remorse' is the one command!" yelled James, followed by Dave's deadly opening solo. It was back to the "Young Metal Attack" now sharpened to a perfect point as the blistering band ripped through another monster. "Anybody here like revenge?" asked James. "This one's called 'Seek and Destroy.'" This was a new destroyer, lengthened and loaded with the heaviest uranium imaginable. This was a masterpiece of a riff. Revenge is sweet!

Then came to the forefront a dimension unimaginable in Ron McGovney's day. "(Anesthesia) Pulling Teeth" featured Mister Burton alone onstage being worshiped by hundreds in total awe of his bass virtuosity. The Rickenbacker wrecker wrought much intensity and after some more wah-wah-wickedness Lars kicked in with his drums, followed by the twin-buzzsaw of Mustaine/Hetfield for the ultimate speedfest: "Whiplash." Most of us needed neck braces long before "Whiplash" started and we certainly didn't need two million beats per minute to finish the job!

"How many of you fuckers are evil?" asked Dave before 'Tallica took on that timeless classic "Am I Evil?". Waves of headbangers bopped and bowed their heads in time to the crunchy rifferama, which James noticed as he switched the lyrics asking the crowd "Are you evil? Yes, YOU are!" Mister Satan would have been proud . . . and why quit after only one Diamond Head song? Metallica then raged into "The Prince" at extreme velocity and then, before we knew it, the show was over!

Actually, the show was not over. The audience chanted and demanded another chestnut, a cover of "Blitzkrieg" by the British band of the same name. It's a short, powerful tune that allowed Dave to really wail some ripping leads, probably the best guitar work that night. The band then propelled into the feedback frenzy and fast guitar riff of fan-favorite "Metal Militia." The crowd went wild! The scene was an onslaught of anarchy until James slowed it down halfway through for the "Metal Up Your Ass" chant while Cliff and Dave exchanged scintillating solos. Soon it was back into the bloody bludgeoning of "Me-TUL ME-Li-SHAAA!!" It was that rip-roaring supersonic screamer that crushed the entire crowd.

Everyone was exhausted and wiped out as the apocalyptic foursome took their bows and headed off for interviews and alcohol. After that cataclysmic concert every true metal fan bought tickets to the next Stone bash two weeks later in hopes of additional ear destruction by the Bay Area's best. Meanwhile Metallica kept busy recording a short new demo featuring two new originals, "No Remorse" and "Whiplash," which was by far their best quality demo to date. Produced by Mark Whittaker at no expense (the demo was a project for his school recording class) the fifth demo soon became known as the "KUSF demo" because we were the first to play it . . . and we played the shit out of it! Then came the ultimate Stone show on March 19 as the boys teamed up with heavy locals Warning and unfortunate headliners Culprit. Warning put on a thundering set, but Culprit, just visiting from Seattle, was visibly out of their league and got blown away by the molten bombast of Metallica. These northerners were a fairly good Iron Maidenish/pre-Queensrÿcheish rocking band but they weren't quite prepared for the violent assault of the vicious San Francisco thrash metal crowd.

Metallica put on an amazing concert, luckily filmed by an amateur crew. Some of the footage wound up on *Cliff 'Em All*. They brought forth a stunningly powerful set to the sold-out thrash metal crowd. There were drunken interviews afterward that the film crew unfortunately missed documenting. I recall Dave Mustaine getting into another drunken fight after that show. Mustaine was an amazing force, more than just a quarter of Metallica; he seemed to be bigger than life onstage (and off), encompassing most of 'Tallica's energy live. But his problems with alcohol began to get overwhelming. Mustaine drank more and faster than anyone else. His edginess provided the perfect metal energy onstage at the Stone combined with the music's forceful power, but offstage afterwards his violent outbursts were legendary and Dave got into altercations after most of the Bay Area gigs. Metallica had taken the Bay Area by storm and was about to embark east to open for their heroes Venom (and others) and record a real record in New Jersey, which would later become the infamous *Kill 'Em All*.

Before Metallica left for the East Coast, Mark Whittaker threw a farewell bash to end all parties. The guys had hired Mark as their manager and he turned the "MetalliMansion" loose before they packed for the trip. Exodus asked me to manage them in his place and I was supposed to fire their bass player (before Gary or Paul would kill him). Little did I know two-fifths of Exodus would soon be gone when Metallica called on Kirk later that next week!

While driving the band's U-Haul east the next few days, Dave went on an extreme bender and almost crashed many times with James, Lars, Cliff and Mark riding in back. At this point, Dave was just too out of control. The band realized Dave was a liability and Kirk Hammett might be the perfect replacement. Dave played a couple gigs in New York in early April and got canned shortly after. Kirk flew in that same day and the band would soon after make its mark in history. It was the end of an era. In a very short six months Metallica had conquered California, as it would soon conquer the world.

Ron Quintana, 2008

My Metallica Experience...Or What I Remember Anyway...

Culprit was signed on to do a song entitled "Players" for *U.S. Metal II*, a compilation record of unsigned bands from around the country on Mike Varney's Shrapnel Records. We had played a couple of times in and around the Bay Area with bands like Exodus and we started to build a buzz and get some press. Around the same time, Metallica was on a compilation album as well with the song "Hit the Lights," if my memory is correct. Some girls I met turned me on to it, but that was about all I knew of Metallica at the time. I thought Metallica was the coolest name I ever heard and it really summed up the whole scene. "Metal Up Your Ass!"

We later went on to record a full-length record on Shrapnel at a studio called Prairie Sun in Cotati, CA. During the recording process Varney had booked us a gig at the Stone in San Francisco with Metallica. I think he was sniffing around trying to get them to sign with him. We started hearing rumors that the Metallica crowd was brutal to their support bands, but I recall us having a really great show and the audience totally digging us as well. There weren't a lot of people at the show, maybe a couple hundred. I remember wearing a purple vest with metal studs I got from Rudy Sarzo and smashing a brand new B.C. Rich bass thinking I was so cool. One of my roadies had to glue it back together so I could finish recording the album because we were so broke! After we finished our set, Dave Mustaine basically threw my guitarist John DeVol's pedals into the corner in a big ball of duct tape. I guess we weren't getting out of their way fast enough. My drummer Bud Burrill grabbed Dave by the neck and there was a little scuffle but Dave was obviously drunk so I can see why they had their problems with him. Needless to say, due to this incident with Dave, we didn't exchange high fives with Metallica after the show.

Metallica was great but quite honestly I didn't really get the speed metal thing at the time (boy was I wrong). We were

from Seattle and nobody was even really doing original music at the time, let alone speed metal. It's not that I didn't like it; I just never really heard anything like it before. It was like punk sped up even faster. Honestly, I spent most of my time talking to Culprit fans after the show so I didn't watch a lot of Metallica that night . . . until I heard that bass! I went flying up to the stage to watch Cliff do the most amazing bass solo (next to Stanley Clarke's) that I had ever seen. It was so awesome. He was the first guy I ever heard use a wah-wah on bass apart from Chris Squire. This guy took it to another level. What a humbling experience for me. I actually thought I was good at the time . . .

Years later I tried out for Metallica and got to play through Cliff's rig. It had to be hard on those guys seeing someone else playing those songs and losing their brother. It was a little uncomfortable for everybody involved. You can't replace a guy like that.

Looking back on the whole thing 25 years later is a trip. I am proud to have been a small part of the West Coast/U.S. metal uprising, but these guys literally changed the world.

Never Enough Thunder,
Scott Earl
Bass — Culprit

Metallica: The Club Dayz is a collection of photographs I shot of the now legendary rock band Metallica between 1982 and 1987. This book contains rare and exclusive photographs from six of the band's earliest performances including their first shows in San Francisco at the Stone and the Old Waldorf. The shows featured the original line up with Dave Mustaine (guitar) and Ron McGovney (bass), Cliff Burton's introductory gig with the band at the Stone, the last San Francisco Metallica show with Dave Mustaine, and Kirk's Metallica debut.

As chief photographer of *Metal Rendezvous International*, a groundbreaking heavy rock magazine that was published throughout the '80s, I was given unlimited access to hang out with and photograph this fledgling metal band. My job at the time was to capture the band live onstage and offstage and provide the magazine with the finest unique photographs of Metallica, whether they featured the band showcasing their brazen live energy in concert, or unveiling some of their crazy and unpredictable offstage antics. I was there with my camera at every one of their early Bay Area shows, live without a photo pit, crushed among the savage crowd as they headbanged fearlessly to their local heroes. It wasn't an easy gig by any means but it was an experience I would treasure forever. And for the very first time I am opening up my photo vault for all of you to witness and visually experience truly one of the greatest rock bands of all-time during their embryonic stage.

Influenced musically by the new breed of British metal yet epitomizing the punk rock attitude, Metallica's loud, snotty and don't-give-a-f*ck attitude is very evident in these photographs. Most of the photos in this book have never been published and many of the images have never before been revealed to the public. I had a blast going though my files and reliving these shows, and working on this book was a truly gratifying experience for me. The time I spent with Metallica back then was one of the greatest experiences of my life. I think everyone who had the fortune of witnessing this band back then knew that Metallica was going to be huge . . . but I don't think anyone could have predicted exactly *how* huge.

I really hope that you, the viewers, enjoy these photographs as much as I enjoyed taking them. You might say that this book is a long-lost chapter of this band's visual history.

Lastly, I must give praise to my old friends who helped me with this book by adding their memories of Metallica during this monumental time! So without any further ado, I present to you, *Metallica: The Club Dayz* . . .

Keep it Heavy, Make it Metal... Aloha,
Bill Hale

09/18/82

Bitch (LA)
Hans Naughty (SF)
Metallica (LA)

The Stone
San Francisco, CA

Hey Bill, shoot THIS! This is probably my first shot of Metallica. Just by looking at James's expression, I knew it wasn't going to be an easy assignment.

Dave Mustaine ripping through another blazing lead.

I believe this was the very first gig where James both sang and played.

The band performed several Diamond Head classics that night. It was, as James would say back then, "Hella-cool!"

James Alan Hetfield

James Hetfield live at the Stone.

Dave Mustaine – lead guitar

Ron McGovney – bass

Ron and his 1982 Washburn B-20.

The "Young Metal Attack."

Lars Ulrich Lars started out as an aspiring tennis player, but after his very first concert in Copenhagen, where he witnessed the extraordinary talent of Deep Purple's Ian Paice, he redirected his life's ambitions and set his sights on being a drummer.

Young, Wild and Untamed Metallica with
the ever-present St. Red. Several years later
Dave got his revenge, choking out
St. Red in another photo session.

Yeah, we're **BAD.** And one day
we are going to rule the **WORLD**!

The Shot Seen 'Round the World This is perhaps my
most famous photograph. A couple of months after this
shoot, Lars asked if I could send him a few pictures to mail
to *Kerrang!* This ended up as one of the most-used Metallica
pics from the early days. It was bootlegged on everything
from patches, posters and CDs to appearing on VH-1.
And no, I never got paid for it.

10/18/82

Lääz Rocket (SF)
Metallica (LA)
Overdrive (SF)

The Old Waldorf
San Francisco, CA

Plotting and Scheming St. Red helps the
band ready the night's set list. "Hmm . . .
'Hit the Lights,' what's next?"

Life Backstage... These next two photos were shot in succession as I quickly panned across the room to capture the action. No posing allowed, just real, candid pix. LEFT: James listening to suggestions for the night's set list. RIGHT: The future rock star in his underwear.

SNARL, SNARL... Dave's look of sheer mental torment as he thumbs through my old photo book. The band could never just pose; they were either flipping me off or contorting their mugs as if I was torturing them.

Flying "V" and Studs A side view of the young star as he tears up "Seek and Destroy."

Live and In Your Face!

The Fast, The Furious and Their Fans The Old Waldorf
was not a large club — there was little room between the
stage, the soundboard and the back wall — so you can
imagine the intensity of the crowd. Metallica was the middle
band that night, which was a pretty big step up, considering
this was only their second gig in San Francisco.

Bleed For Me, San Francisco

There wasn't a doubt in anyone's mind that Dave was already an accomplished guitarist.

Pure Mustaine! This photo shows Dave in full shred-mode. Truly a "Guitar God" in training!

Crash — Bang Here is a rare photo of Lars behind
his kit. You can tell he is thoroughly exhausted toward
the end of Metallica's blistering hour-long set. Lars set
the standard for high-performance speed metal.

Smile PLEASE! This is the second time I attempted a candid group shot. It was a challenge to get the whole band to stand together, but I believe I captured a special moment here. The rag in Lars's mouth is a copy of K.J. Doughton's fanzine, *Northwest Metal*. It was fellow metal fan Brian Lew who brought the fanzine to the band and it started the tradition of Metallica being photographed with their favorite fanzines.

Aaarrggghhh! This was the last shot
of the session. You can already see that
Ron wasn't quite fitting in with the rest
of the bunch. Certainly, the cracks were
beginning to show, as James, Dave and
Lars were usually over-the-top, whereas
Ron was much more conventional.

11/29/82

Metallica (LA)
Vicious Rumors (SF)
Exodus (SF)

The Old Waldorf
San Francisco, CA
(Headliners at last...)

**Live, Raw and Without a Photo Pit!
Part I** This 1982 shot is the quintessential
Metallica at the Old Waldorf photo. It cap-
tures the true spirit of the emergence of Bay
Area thrash metal, which created unity
between rabid fans and the band.

Motorbreath James was much more confident with his role in the band at this point, though Dave still did most of the talking between songs.

Dave Wowing the Old Waldorf Crowd

Arguably, Dave Mustaine was the originator of "thrash metal" guitar riffs. The photos on the opposite page show just how innovative Dave's playing was. Notice, as he approaches the front row, how the fans stop banging their heads for a brief moment to focus on his lightning-fast hands!

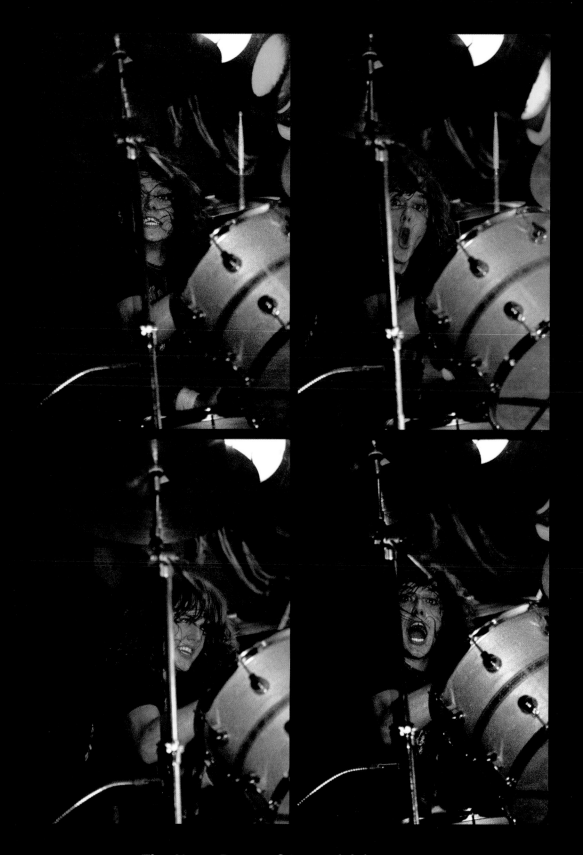

The Many Faces of Lars Ulrich

Stage Left... Stage Right...

03/05/83

Metallica (SF)
Lääz Rockit (SF)
Exodus (SF)

The Stone
San Francisco, CA
(Cliff's first gig)

Now playing bass for Metallica, I give you . . .
Cliff Burton! Dave and Cliff pose for the camera
before Cliff's first show with the Metal Militia.

Do you know where this plug has been? Cliff attempts to tune his bass before his first gig with the band.

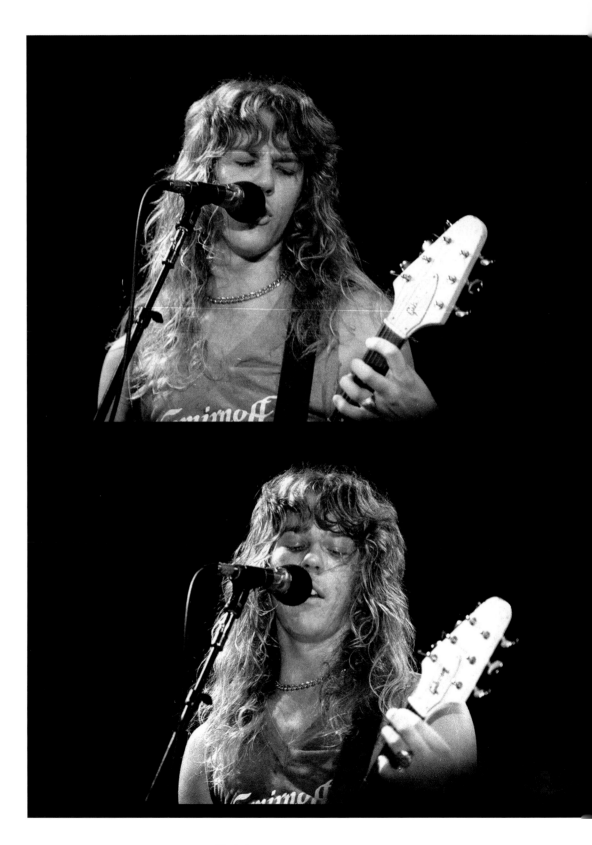

James Hetfield live at the Stone.

Cheers! The infamous middle finger,
exposed tongue and guitar.

Two of the most influential guitarists of the '80s Yes, that's Dave with little Kirk Hammett, backstage at the Stone.

Lars and Paul Lars sports his Heavy Metal
blue denim vest while Exodus's Paul Baloff
flaunts his bangs.

**Live, Raw and Without a Photo Pit!
Part II** A view from the crowd of Exodus's
Kirk Hammett.

EXODUS Quick guys, can I get a group shot? (Clockwise from the top) Geoff Andrews, Paul Baloff, Kirk Hammett, Tom Hunting and Gary Holt. Thanks, guys . . . now go rage!

THIS PAGE: *Metal Mania*'s founding editor Mr. Ron Quintana. Ron not only started *Metal Mania* but was one of the first metal DJs in the Bay Area and is still a KUSF mainstay.

OPPOSITE PAGE: Dave, James and Cliff in action. That is early Metallica roadie Bob Gamber in the bottom left shot discussing the weather with Dave. Bob is the owner of Vinyl Revolution, a very cool record store in Monterey, CA. If you are ever in the area, stop on by and tell Bob that Bill sent ya! (Yes, a shameless plug for an old friend!)

Ron Quintana with James and Dave...
As Ron would always say, "My shirt's cooler!"

Dave in the middle of one of his infamous rants . . .
We are Metallica and we play **ROCK & ROLL!**
No, wait . . . that's Motörhead.

The Stone TOP: A flyer for the gig.
BOTTOM: This is the front lobby of the
Stone . . . In the middle of the frame
you can see Dave Mustaine and fellow
Bay Area metal photographer Harold O
chatting with Exodus's Kirk Hammett.

0 3 / 1 9 / 8 3

Metallica (SF)
Culprit (Seattle)
Warning (SF)

The Stone
San Francisco, CA
(Their best gig yet!)

The Leader of the Metal Militia Don't
ask me what I said to James to make him sit
still. This was one band that never stood still,
not even for a second!

The Man Who Would Be King This shot may have inspired British photographer Robert Ellis, who years later captured Lars behind his drum kit during the Day On the Green Festival — a much sought-after photo that was featured on the back cover of *Master of Puppets*.

Standing in the Shadows Cliff watches from
the opposite end of the stage as James and Dave
whip the crowd into a frenzy.

Cliff, Onstage at the Stone Cliff quickly clicked with Lars and the band. At this point, Metallica was on top of the world. Cliff had been the missing part of the puzzle.

Cliff Here's yet another great side view shot of Cliff sporting his trademark denim jacket, bell-bottom jeans and trusty 1973 Rickenbacker 4001.

Live, Raw and Without a Photo Pit!
Part III As soon as Metallica hit the stage
there was no doubt in anybody's mind that
this was the best heavy metal band in the
world. Cliff, James, Dave and Lars ripped
the Stone apart that night!

The Night of the Banging Head The Stone
was never to be the same again!

Back to Back... I love this shot
of Dave and Cliff! They were giving
the jam-packed crowd at the Stone
that night one of the most intense
shows I've ever witnessed.

METAL UP YOUR ASS!!! James tears into what would later become a Metallica classic. By this time, James was nearly in full lead-singer mode.

Right Back at You! James gets his revenge on an unwitting member of the crowd.

Say Cheese... This would be one of my last attempts
at a great Metallica group shot. And I almost got it.

The Shot! Second time's a charm. I had told the guys, "Please, let's keep this cool" . . . and the untamed lads actually complied!

YEAH, RIGHT! Lars hated this shot but I thought
this totally captured the untapped energy that was
Metallica . . . pure, raw and in your face!

OUCH! Could this be the real reason Dave was fired?

James, Lars & Dave Just one year
previously I captured the band in a very
similar photograph against that very
same wall. Dave flipped me off in that
shot as well.

Mister Varney Here's a rare photo of Shrapnel
Records founder Mike Varney (pictured beside Ron
Quintana), who sought to sign Metallica to his
record label — to no avail.

Cliff Burton, Dave Mustaine and Friend This shot was taken just a few doors down from the Stone in San Francisco. I love this photograph for three reasons: First, it shows the warmth and compassion between true friends. Second, it is the end of innocence, as in the not-so-distant future Dave would be out of the band, and Cliff would be gone forever. Finally, it's just a great shot!

Cliff, a Friend and Dave just being Dave! Truth be told, Dave was my favorite member of the band. He was always a riot.

Metallica Was Here! I'm not sure if it was one of the opening bands that smashed the glass on the marquee or if it was just a hyped-up fan. Metallica's crowd has the tendency to get a bit riled up after a show!

09/03/83

Raven (UK)
Metallica (SF)
Tourist (SF)

The Stone
San Francisco, CA
(Welcome home, Kirk...)

Live, Raw and Without a Photo Pit! Part IV

This Stone gig was bittersweet for me. I'd shot Metallica since their very first show in San Francisco. I knew all the band members well, but I was closest with Dave. So when I heard that Metallica had fired Dave, I was shocked! There was no doubt that Mr. Hammett would be able to fill the lead guitar slot, but it was Dave who had been the "in-your-face" member of Metallica. St. Red and I decided to place Metallica on the cover of *Metal Rendezvous International*. So, armed with my trusty Nikon, I proceeded to the show, wondering what Metallica would sound like without Dave Mustaine. After the gig, I knew that it wouldn't be long before Metallica would take over the planet! I would still hang out at gigs with them, talk about metal and get the occasional snapshot, but my photographer's intuition told me my time working with Metallica had come to an end.

Blood, Sweat and Cheers This was Kirk's first gig with the band in San Francisco. As you can tell by sweat on Kirk's shirt, it was an oven onstage. Metallica was right on and their fans knew it.

The Major Rager! I remember seeing Cliff's previous band Trauma and thinking to myself, "This bassist just does not fit this mold." But with Metallica, Cliff really came into his own!

Clifford Lee Burton

Pulling Teeth This was shot during Cliff's awesome bass solo.

"The Somber Side of James" It looks like James was caught in a soulful moment. I cannot recall what song James was singing at the time, but it certainly does not look very metal.

Another view from the crowd... Lars photographed from the floor of the Stone.

The Phantom Lord James looking like a true rock star!
I went to this gig for a cover shot, and this seemed to be
the obvious choice.

Loitering, Hanging Out and Just Plain Silliness

Candid Photos...

Jason Curtis Newsted I knew of Jason from his great work with Flotsam and Jetsam. This photo was taken just days after the guys picked him to join the band. One night after a gig at the Stone, I asked Jason to pose as though he was playing the Hammond organ. Jason took it one step further and posted a sign above the organ that read, "Bach!"

Phantasm Phantasm was Ron McGovney's
post-Metallica project with Katon W. De Pena
of Hirax. This band was short-lived but there
are some demos and a great live recording
floating about. This photo was taken in
Los Angeles in April 1987.

ABOVE: The members of Necros pose with James
(please, no more photos!) BELOW: Dave Prichard and
Joey Vera from Armored Saint pose with Kirk and
Mike Coons (Lääz Rockit). The gang is caught
hamming it up backstage after the monstrous
Day on the Green show (08/31/85).

This was to be the last time that I saw Cliff alive... I apologize for the poor photo quality but this is a meaningful image as Dave and Cliff were rarely caught photographed together after Dave was out of the band. Megadeth had opened for King Diamond at the Stone and Cliff was hanging out backstage. Dave and Cliff seemed to be on great terms, like brothers who hadn't seen each other in years. Gone for a moment was any of the animosity of the Metallica / Megadeth rivalry. (L to R) Timi 'Grabber' Hansen, Ole Bang (King Diamond and Mercyful Fate's manager), Mega Dave and Cliff. (San Francisco, 08/12/86)

Cheers! Backstage at Wolfgang's. Uli Roth's Electric Sun just finished performing a stellar set at their San Francisco debut. (L to R) David Godfrey (Heathen), Marc Biedermann (Blind Illusion), Uli Jon Roth and Kirk Hammett.

Carla, Dave and Lars Carla, a friend and
guitarist for Malibu Barbi, pictured laughing it
up with Dave and Lars. This was taken at the
Keystone Berkeley after a Girlschool gig.

Lars & Friends

TOP LEFT: Lars helps Joey Vera with his nasal problem; TOP RIGHT: Lars hanging with St. Red; CENTER: Lars snarling off with Gonzo from Armored Saint; BOTTOM: Lars with Armored Saint guitarist Dave Prichard (R.I.P.)

Cliff Giving a Helping Finger (as James tries to hide).
I remember Cliff asking if I would like to take a picture just
before he gracefully displayed the international hand signal
for "Have a nice day" . . . wasn't that nice of him?

Lars and His Future Faithful Graciously signing
autographs after an Iron Maiden show. As you can see,
Lars doesn't look much older than his fans. (San Jose
Civic, San Jose, CA, 7/3/85)